Building Words

Reproducible Activity Sheets for Grades 2-3

Troll Associates

Troll Teacher Time Savers provide a quick source of self-contained lessons and practice material, designed to be used as full-scale lessons or to make productive use of those precious extra minutes that sometimes turn up in the day's schedule.

Troll Teacher Time Savers can help you to prepare a made-to-order program for your students. Select the sequence of Time Savers that will meet your students' needs, and make as many photocopies of each page as you require. Since Time Savers include progressive levels of complexity and difficulty in each book, it is possible to individualize instruction, matching the needs of each student.

Those who need extra practice and reinforcement for catching up in their skills can benefit from Troll Teacher Time Savers, while other students can use Time Savers for enrichment or as a refresher for skills in which they haven't had recent practice. Time Savers can also be used to diagnose a student's knowledge and skills level, in order to see where extra practice is needed.

Time Savers can be used as homework assignments, classroom or small-group activities, shared learning with partners, or practice for standardized testing. See "Answer Key & Skills Index" to find the specific skill featured in each activity.

ANSWER KEY & SKILLS INDEX

Page 1, **Window Words:** l; g; p; r. **(spelling)**

Page 2, **Let's Build Words:** kitten; button; hidden. **(word parts)**

Page 3, **The Right Brush:** 1-green; 2-drop; 3-thing; 4-black; 5-green; 6-drop; 7-spot; 8-black. **(blends)**

Page 4, **Grandpa's Hat:** 1-ch; 2-th; 3-ld; 4-rd; 5-lt; 6-sh. **(final blends)**

Page 5, **Mystery Words:** 1-nail; 2-table; 3-clock; 4-shoe; 5-saw; 6-mitten. **(definitions)**

Page 6, **More Mystery Words:** 1-your nose; 2-a road; 3-a candle; 4-a written letter; 5-a coat of paint; 6-a towel. **(homophones)**

Page 7, **Two by Two:** bread & butter; shovel & pail; pencil & paper; lock & key; hammer & nails; chair & table. **(logical combinations)**

Page 8, **What's Wrong Here?:** zoo written backwards; girl in cage; mouse says meow; tiger's missing ear; giraffe's trunk; zebra's tail; lion pond; bear's rabbit ear. **(concentration)**

Page 9, **Find the Mistakes:** Wensday; clock; dog; kni; bird; skates; cut-off pant leg; fish; paint brush; 7. **(concentration)**

Page 10, **Picture Words:** cat; lion; deer; zebra. **(spelling)**

Page 11, **More Picture Words:** poke; game; clown; party. **(spelling)**

Page 12, **Reading Secret Messages:** Come here fast; I am on my way. **(spelling)**

Page 13, **Build a House:** 1-rain; 2-barn; 3-farm; 4-rain; 5-farm; 6-barn. **(spelling)**

Page 14, **Tree House Fun:** 1-horn; 2-corn; 3-born; 4-torn; 5-born; 6-corn; 7-horn; 8-torn. **(spelling)**

Page 15, **Nuts & Bolts:** 1-frog; 2-drink; 3-sheep; 4-plant; frog, drink, sheep, plant. **(blends)**

Page 55, **What Is the Question?:** Answers will vary. **(punctuation)**

Page 56, **Question Magic:** 2-Is your mother at work today?; 3-Are there four donkeys in the yard?; 4-Didn't the children want to take their frogs to school?; 5-Are you going to take us to the zoo today?; 6-Are these funny little apples good to eat?; 7-Didn't the scarecrow keep the crows away?; 8-Can Barbara really jump over a high fence? **(query sentences)**

Page 57, **Sentence Time:** Answers will vary. **(writing)**

Page 58, **Exclamation!:** 1-Oh, she's falling!; 2-It was a shiny new bike for Timmy! **(punctuation)**

Page 59, **Who's Talking?:** 1-Eddie; 2-Nancy; 3-yes; 4-no; 5-"meow." **(punctuation)**

Page 60, **The Names Are the Same:** 1-Jill; 2-Kathy; 3-Luis; 4-Richard; 5-Lisa; 6-Duke. **(proper nouns)**

Page 61, **How It Looks, Feels, and Sounds:** 1-hard; 2-bright; 3-cold; 4-high; 5-loud; 6-soft; 7-feels; 8-looks; 9-feels; 10-looks; 11-sounds; 12-feels. **(adjectives)**

Page 62, **Pick the Right Word:** 1-blue; 2-tiny; 3-warm; 4-deep; 5-huge; 6-round; 7-small yellow; 8-dirty, wide; 9-tall, sharp; 10-ugly purple; 11-flat, heavy; 12-orange, long. **(adjectives)**

Page 63, **Star Paste-Up:** 1-b; 2-a; 3-b; 4-b; 5-a; 6-a. **(grammar)**

Page 64, **Right or Wrong?:** 1-b; 2-b; 3-a; 4-a; 5-b; 6-a; 7-b; 8-b. **(grammar)**

Page 65, **What's the Message?:** 1-the dog; 2-the bone; 3-3; 4-4; 5-the girl; 6-the horse; 7-7; 8-8. **(grammar)**

Page 66, **Mixed Match-Ups:** **(metaphors)**

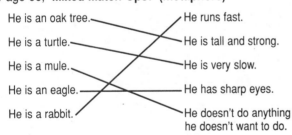

Page 67, **Fill in the Blanks:** 1-hard; 2-quiet; 3-red; 4-sweet; 5-white; 6-gentle; 7-deep; 8-silly; 9-green; 10-slowly. **(similes)**

Page 68, **Same or Different:** 1-a; 2-b; 3-b; 4-a; 5-b. **(metaphors)**

Page 69, **Sentence Fun:** Answers will vary. **(similes)**

Page 70, **Think & Write:** Answers will vary. **(similes and metaphors)**

Page 71, **The Strange Planet:** Answers will vary. **(creative writing)**

Page 72, **Make Up a Story:** Answers will vary. **(creative writing)**

Page 73, **Let's Play:** Answers will vary. **(creative writing)**

Page 74, **The Birthday Party:** Answers will vary. **(creative writing)**

Window Words

Cut out the letters at the bottom of the page. Paste them in the empty "windows" so that they make words across the building.

Name_____ **Date** _____

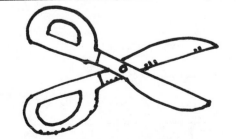  

1

Let's Build Words

You can make a long word from the short words on two of these hammers.

Write the word here. _____

You can make a long word from the short words on two of these saws.

Write the word here. _____

You can make a long word from the short words on two of these screwdrivers.

Write the word here. _____

Name_____ Date _____

The Right Brush

The painter is ready to paint the house. Help her find the right brush for each paint can. Look at the letters on each brush. Then look at the letters on the cans. Match each brush with a can to make a word. Then color that brush and can the same color. Use a different color for each word.

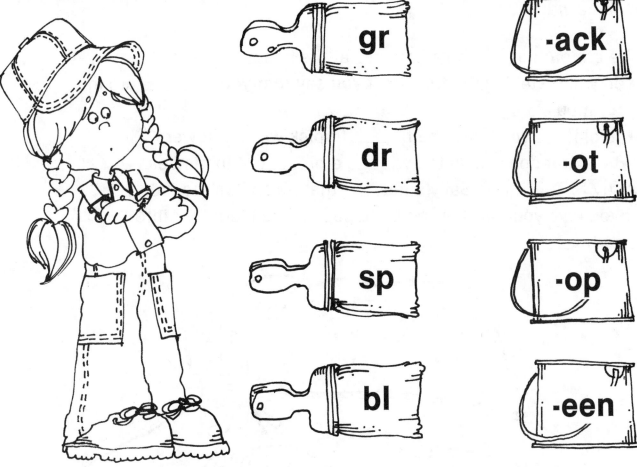

What words did you make? Write them on the lines.

1. _____   2. _____

3. _____   4. _____

Read the sentences below. Pick the word from above that fits in each sentence. Write that word on the line.

5. We ran and played on the _____ grass.

6. Did you _____ your book on the floor?

7. I don't know what that funny _____ is.

8. That little _____ dog is so pretty.

Name_____ Date _____

3

Grandpa's Hat

Read sentence 1. Then look at the word endings on Grandpa's hat. One ending will finish all the words in sentence 1. Find that ending and write it in the spaces to finish the words. Then do the other sentences the same way.

1. We ate our lun_____ on a ben_____ at the bea_____.
2. You will be telling the tru_____ if you say that your tee_____ are in your mou_____.
3. The chi_____ went into the fie_____ to pick wi_____ flowers.
4. When Grandpa was in the ya_____, a bi_____ got in his bea_____.
5. Andy fe_____ it was Sally's fau_____ that he spilled the sa_____.
6. If you give your brother too big a pu_____, he'll cra_____ into that bu_____.

-ld   -ch   -th
-rd   -sh   -lt

Name_____ Date _____

4

Mystery Words

Read each riddle. Then look at the pictures at the bottom of the page. Cut out the pictures. Attach them in the spaces so they tell the answers to the riddles.

1.
I have a head,
but I never think.
What am I?

Attach here.

4.
I have a tongue,
but I can't talk.
What am I?

Attach here.

2.
I have legs,
but I can't walk.
What am I?

Attach here.

5.
I have sharp
teeth, but I
can't eat.
What am I?

Attach here.

3.
I have a face,
but I never smile.
What am I?

Attach here.

6.
I have a thumb,
but I have no
fingers.
What am I?

Attach here.

Name_____

Date _____

Cut along dotted lines.

More Mystery Words

Read each riddle. Then look at the pictures at the bottom of the page. Cut out the pictures and attach each one in a space so that it tells the answer to the riddle.

1. What smells the most in your kitchen?

Attach here.

4. What letter can you never find in the alphabet?

Attach here.

2. What takes you places but never moves at all?

Attach here.

5. What kind of coat doesn't keep you warm?

Attach here.

3. The longer I go, the shorter I grow. What am I?

Attach here.

6. The more I dry, the wetter I get. What am I?

Attach here.

Name_____ **Date** _____

 Cut along dotted lines.

  Dear Pat,  HERS

Two by Two

Two different things often go together. Look at the pictures on the left. Then find the picture on the right that goes with each one on the left—like bread and butter. Draw a line to connect the two pictures.

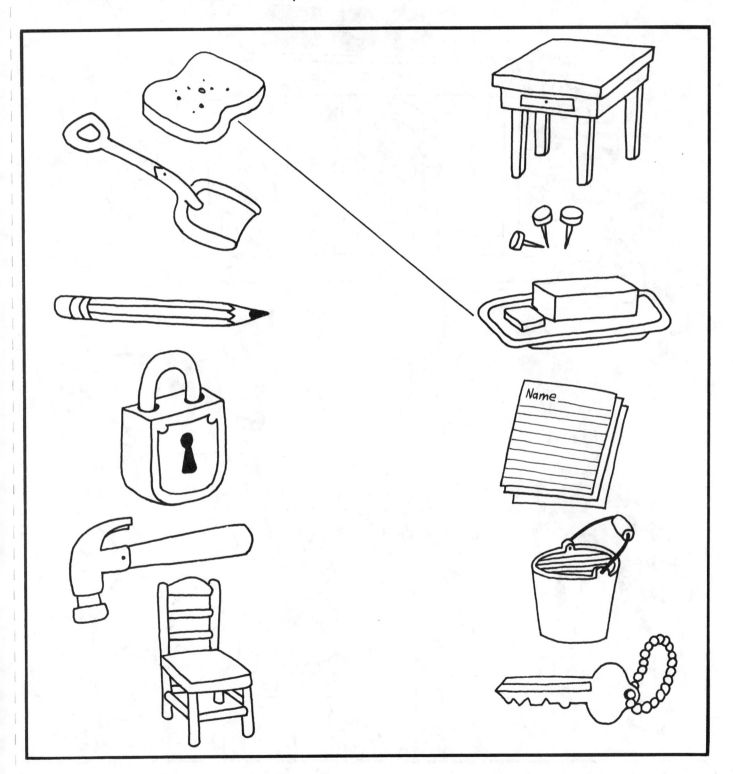

What's Wrong Here?

There are **eight** things wrong in this picture. Can you find them?
Make an X on each thing that is wrong.

Name_____ Date _____

Find the Mistakes

There are **ten** things wrong in this picture. Can you find them?
Make an X on each thing that is wrong.

Name_____ Date _____

9

Picture Words

Look at each picture. Say its name. Write the first letter of each picture name on the line under the picture. The letters will make a word. Write out the answer. See example below.

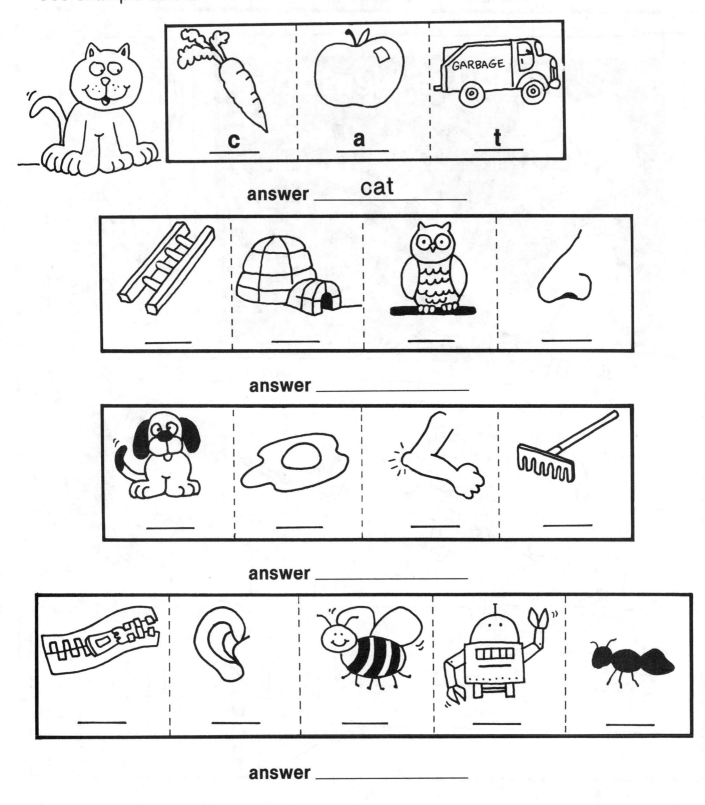

c   a   t

answer _____cat_____

answer _____

answer _____

answer _____

Name _____ **Date** _____

10

More Picture Words

Look at each picture. Say its name. Write the first letter of each picture name on the line under the picture. The letters will make a word. Write out the answers.

answer _____

answer _____

answer _____

answer _____

Name_____ Date _____

Reading Secret Messages

What do these messages say? To find out, write the first letter of the first word in the first space. Write the first letter of the second word in the second space, and so on. Make the first letter of the message a capital letter. Look at this example.

Chirp

<u>R</u>obins <u>u</u>se <u>n</u>ests.

$\underline{\text{R}}$ $\underline{\text{u}}$ $\underline{\text{n}}$!
1   2   3

The message is "Run!"

Jamal sent a secret message to Jenny.
Can you figure it out?

Clever owls make
everything. Help each
rabbit eat. Five
apples sang today.

___ ___ ___ ___   ___ ___ ___ ___   ___ ___ ___ ___!
1   2   3   4   5   6   7   8   9   10   11   12

Jenny sent the message below to Jamal.
What does it say?

I'll ask monkeys.
Open no mail yet.
We always yell.

___ ___ ___   ___ ___   ___ ___   ___ ___ ___.
1   2   3   4   5   6   7   8   9   10

Name_____ Date _____

Build a House

These men are building a house. Help them choose the best pieces of wood for the job. Look at the letter on each piece of wood. Then draw a line from the letter to the letters on the house to make a word. One has already been done for you.

What words did you make? Write them on the lines.

1._____ 2._____ 3._____

Read each sentence below. Choose the word from above that fits in each sentence. Write that word on the line.

4. The _____ came down and got us all wet.

5. The Smiths grow corn on their _____.

6. We opened the _____ door and let the horses out.

Name_____ **Date** _____

13

Tree House Fun

The children are putting a roof on their tree house. But they don't need all the wood. Look at the letter on each piece of wood. Find the letters that make words when put in front of **-orn**. Draw a line from each letter to the roof.

g
h
c
b
d
t

-orn

What words did you make? Write them on the lines.

1. _____   2. _____

3. _____   4. _____

Read each sentence below. Pick the word from above that fits in each sentence. Write the word on the line.

5. The day you were _____ is your birthday.

6. We like to eat _____ tortillas.

7. Little Boy Blue, come blow your _____ .

8. John's shirt got _____ when he fell from his bike.

Name_____ Date _____

14

Nuts & Bolts

Match the nuts 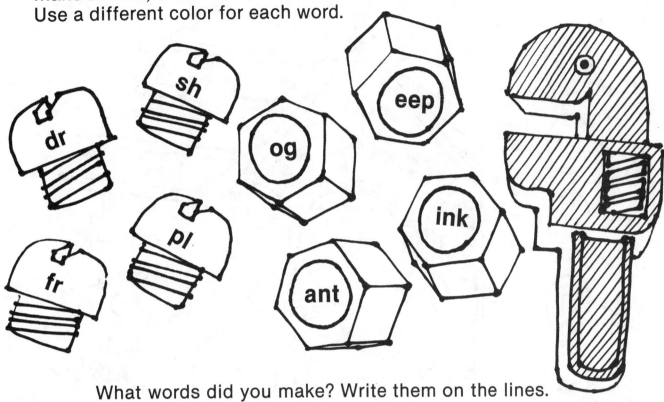 with the bolts . Look at the letters on each bolt. Then look at the letters on each nut. If the letters make a word, color the nut and bolt the same color. Use a different color for each word.

What words did you make? Write them on the lines.

1. _____   2. _____

3. _____   4. _____

Look at the pictures below.
Pick the word from above that best fits each picture.
Write the word under the picture.

_____   _____   _____   _____

Name_____ Date _____

15

A New Home

Three nails will finish the birdhouse. Look at the letters on each nail. Find the letters that make a word when put in front of **-ip**. Then draw a line from each nail to the birdhouse to make a word.

What words did you make? Write them on the lines.

1. _____   2. _____   3. _____

Read each sentence. Then circle the word that fits in each sentence.

4. I like to **(ship , skip)** down the street with my friends.

5. I saw a **(ship , slip)** in the deep water.

6. I walked slowly so I would not **(slip , ship)** on the ice.

Name_____ Date _____

16

You Name It

Look at the pictures below. Choose the letter at the bottom of the page that finishes each picture name. Then write that letter on the line. Read the words.

chie____

clu____

chai____

screa____

carro____

mi____

soc____

whee____

t l x b r k f m

Name_____ Date _____

Carmen's Boats

Look at the word parts on the left. Then look at the word parts on the right. Draw a line from each part on the left to the part on the right that completes each word.

min

num

win

sup

ber

per

ute

ter

Write the words you made.

1. _____

2. _____

3. _____

4. _____

Can You Read This?

Jenny has a new idea for making secret messages. When you see a word, write the first letter of the word on the line. When you see a picture, write the first letter of the name of the picture on the line. Start each message with a capital letter. See example below.

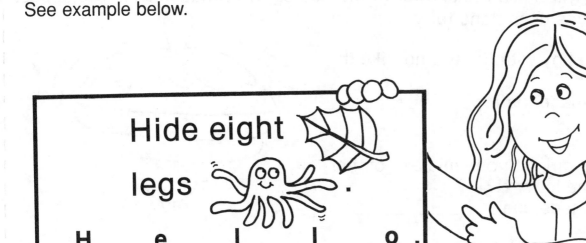

Hide eight legs .

H	e	l	l	o	.
1	2	3	4	5	

What does this message say? →

Catch another .
Your understood.
Ride east around
. The
is silly.

1	2	3
4	5	6
7	8	9	10
11	12	13	14

?

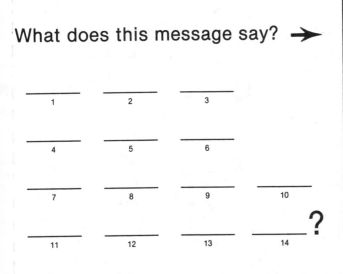

Nibble our .
It's at night.

1	2	3	4	5	6	7

!

Name_____ Date _____

19

Letter Riddles

Read each riddle. Then look at the words at the bottom of the page. Pick out the word that will finish the answer to the riddle. Write that word in the space. The first one has been done for you.

1. Why did the boy with the top not like the letter **S**?
   Because it made the **top** _____stop_____.

2. Why did the girl with one mistake on her paper like the letter **N**?
   Because it made **one** _____.

3. Why does the boy whose shirt is too small like the letter **F**?
   Because it makes **it** _____.

4. How did the letter **S** help the girl train her dog?
   By making **it** _____.

5. Why is the letter **N** a help in hot weather?
   Because it makes **ice** _____.

6. Why does a man who is losing his hair like the letter **H**?
   Because it makes **air** _____.

    fit   **hair**   **stop**   **sit**   **nice**   **none**

Name_____ Date _____

Fun on the Farm

Look at the word beginnings on the list at the left. Then look at the word parts on the barn. Finish each word on the left by writing the correct word part on the line. Use each word part three times.

tur _____

wag _____

mon _____

cray _____

thun _____

don _____

spi _____

drag _____

lad _____

-on

-key

-der

Look at the pictures below.
Choose a word from the list above that fits each picture.
Write the word on the line under the picture.

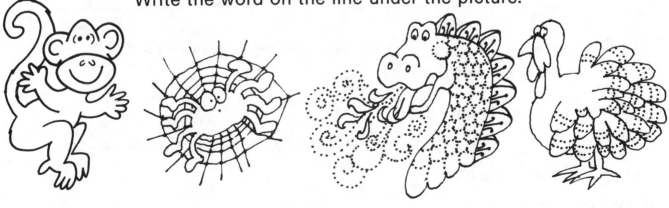

_____ _____ _____ _____

Name_____ Date _____

21

A Name Game

These workers got their hats all mixed up. Look at the names under
the workers. Then look at the letters on the hats. Draw a line from
each name to a hat so it makes a word.

What words did you make? Write them on the lines.

1. _____   2. _____   3. _____

4. _____   5. _____   6. _____

Read the sentences. Then pick a word from the above list that fits in
each space. Write the word where it should go.

7. The river runs through a deep green _____ .

8. With a _____ , some sugar, and water, you can make a

    good drink and sell it for a _____ .

9. I wonder what will _____ tomorrow.

10. Which animal do you like_____ , a squirrel or a _____ ?

Name_____ Date _____

Word Tricks

Sometimes you can move the letters of a word around to make a new word. Read each sentence below. To find the word that goes in each space, change the letters of the word under the line. Write the new word in the space.

Sentence 1 has been done for you.

1. Please whisper the secret in my _____ear_____.
   are

2. Ann has a golden _____ on her finger.
   grin

3. The big bike _____ will start in five minutes.
   care

4. Watch your _____ when you come down the stairs.
   pets

5. Juan set the fox free from the _____ .
   part

6. Write your _____ at the top of the paper.
   mean

7. The firefighters used a _____ to put out the fire.
   shoe

8. A wise old _____ has a _____ in this tree.
   low   **sent**

Name_____ Date _____

More Word Tricks

Sometimes you can switch the letters of a word to make a new word. Sometimes the same letters will make several different words. Look at the underlined words in the sentence below.

Ann made cookies to **eat** with her **tea,** but I **ate** them all up.

All three words are made from the same letters—a, e, and t.
Each story below has words in it that are made from the same letters.
Look at the first underlined word in each story. Change the letters around
to find the word that fits in each of the spaces. Write the words.

1. Jane's dog Skippy **won** first prize at the dog
show. Her cat was the best in the cat show, too.
So _____ Jane has two blue ribbons.
She is glad to _____ such special pets.

2. **Dear** David,
    When you _____ this letter, you will be
    surprised. I learned to dive. I can even dive off
    the high board. Did you ever think I would _____
    to do such a scary thing?
                    Your friend,
                    Bob

3. Our class planted flowers. We needed a lot of **pots**. We put them near
the windows. That was a good _____ for them. They grew so tall
the _____ were as high as our heads. If they don't
_____ soon, they will be up to the ceiling.

Name_____ Date _____

Paint & Brush

Some words seem to go together, like paint and brush. Look at the words on the paint can below. Then find the word on the brush at the bottom of the page that goes with the word on the paint can. Write the word in the space.

1. **lost** and _____
2. **name** and _____
3. **pots** and _____
4. **bacon** and _____
5. **socks** and _____
6. **king** and _____
7. **bow** and _____
8. **salt** and _____
9. **needle** and _____
10. **thunder** and _____

Color this picture
when you finish
putting in the answers.

shoes	arrow
queen	address
pepper	lightning
found	eggs
pans	thread

Name_____ Date _____

25

Two In One

Some big words are made up of two smaller words. Look at the sample in the box at the right. Then look at the words below. Make a line in the middle of the word to show where it should be cut. Use the smaller words to fill in the spaces in each sentence.

base|ball

When we play *baseball*, we hit the ___**ball**___ and run to the ___**base**___.

1. **tea spoon**

A *teaspoon* is a small _____ used for stirring _____ .

2. **earth worm**

An *earthworm* is a _____ that lives in the _____ .

3. **foot print**

A *footprint* in the mud is a _____ made by a _____ .

4. **mail box**

A *mailbox* is a _____ we put our _____ in.

5. **snow storm**

When _____ falls during a _____ , we have a *snowstorm.*

6. **sail boat**

A *sailboat* is a _____ with a _____ .

Tom's Tugboats

bed

blue

camp

grass

note

rattle

berry

fire

room

snake

hopper

book

Tom makes toy tugboats.
You can see that **tugboat** is made from two smaller words, **tug** and **boat**. Look at the boat parts on the left. Then look at the parts on the right. Draw a line from each part on the left to a part on the right so the smaller words make another word.

Write the words you made.

1._____

2._____

3._____

4._____

5._____

6._____

Make a Story

Read the story and fill in the missing words on the lines under the boxes. The picture clues will help you.

Kim and Paul went for a walk to find a pot of gold.

They saw a  in the air. They saw a

_____ _____

growing in a garden.   They saw a  swimming in a pond.

_____

It rained a little, and they saw a . But they did not find a

_____

pot of gold.   On their way home, they found a lucky

_____

They were very happy, so they climbed up to their

_____

They ate two  each. "Yummy, that was better than a

_____

pot of gold," said Paul. Kim agreed.

Go-Cart Fun

Wendy and Steve are building go-carts. Each of them needs four wheels. Pick out four wheels for Wendy that make words when **-ing** is added. Color them green. Then pick out four wheels for Steve that make words when **-ly** is added. Color them orange. Make an X on the wheel you don't use.

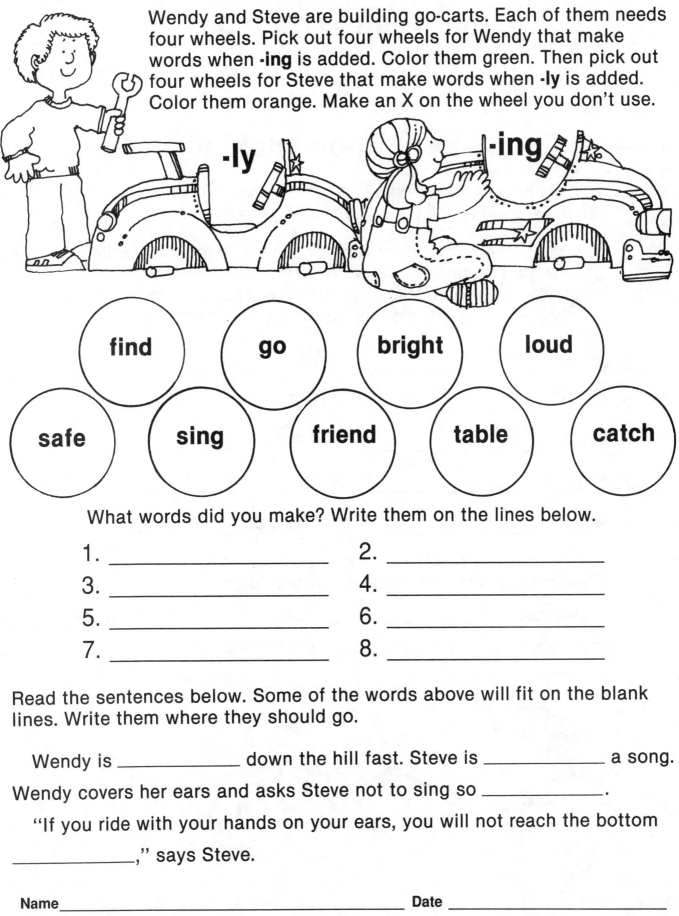

What words did you make? Write them on the lines below.

1. _____   2. _____
3. _____   4. _____
5. _____   6. _____
7. _____   8. _____

Read the sentences below. Some of the words above will fit on the blank lines. Write them where they should go.

Wendy is _____ down the hill fast. Steve is _____ a song.

Wendy covers her ears and asks Steve not to sing so _____.

"If you ride with your hands on your ears, you will not reach the bottom _____," says Steve.

Name_____   Date _____

29

Word Addition

run + ing = run(n)ing

Look at the word *run.* Then look at the word *running.*
Before we could add *-ing* we had to add another letter.

make + ing = making

Look at the word *make.* Then look at the word *making.*
Before we could add *-ing* we had to take away the letter *e.*

Now look at the words below. Add *-ing* to each of them and write
the new word on the line. You will have to add letters to four
words. You will have to take away the letter *e* from six words.
Use the examples above to help you change the words below.

1. **give** _____ 2. **fit** _____

3. **race** _____ 4. **leave** _____

5. **step** _____ 6. **smile** _____

7. **chase** _____ 8. **swim** _____

9. **win** _____ 10. **dance** _____

Some of the words you made above will fit in the spaces in the
following story. Write them where they should go.

   As Carlos was _____ his house one morning, he saw

two of his friends _____ past on their bikes. He

wondered which one was _____ the race.

Make a New Word

Write **-un** in front of each of the words below to make a new word.
Then draw a line from the new word to the picture that goes with it.

_____lock

_____button

_____wrap

_____dress

_____happy

_____tied

Read the sentences. The words you made above will fit in the spaces.
Write them where they should go.

1. Greg couldn't wait to _____ his birthday gifts.

2. Ann can't _____ for bed because she can't _____ her shirt

   or get her shoes _____.

3. Peter is _____ because he lost his key and can't _____ the door.

Name_____ **Date** _____

Four Dogs

Read the words below. Then draw a line from each word on the left to the one on the right that sounds just like it.

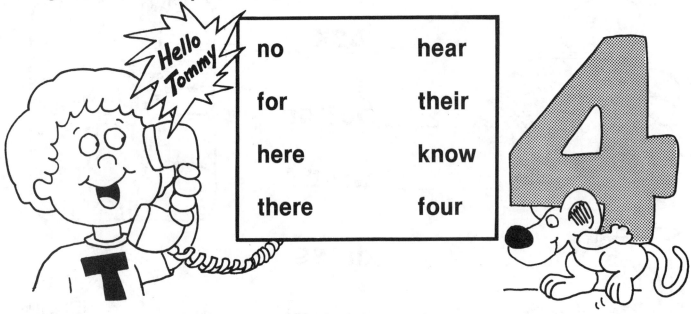

Hello Tommy

no	hear
for	their
here	know
there	four

Read the sentences below. In each sentence, circle the two words that sound the same, but look different and mean different things.

1. Heather ate four hot dogs for dinner.

2. They lost their way and got there late.

3. Does Pam know there is no school today?

4. You can hear better if you sit here in front.

This is #4, and I could even eat more.

Name_____ Date _____

First in Line

Look at the two words in each box. Then look at the two sentences below the box. Write each word in the sentence where it fits.

be	bee

I'm first!

1. A _____ flew right in my window.

2. Jill wanted to _____ first in line.

by	buy

CANDY 10¢

Yuckies

3. Sue didn't _____ any candy.

4. Mike rode _____ on a brown pony.

see	sea

I found them!

5. Did you _____ my shoes anywhere?

6. Many kinds of fish live in the _____.

Name_____   Date_____

Time to Read

Read the words below. Then draw a line from each word on the left to the one on the right that sounds just like it.

red	rode
road	eye
I	write
right	read

Hi! I can see you with my right eye.

Read the sentences below. In each sentence, circle the two words that look different and mean different things but sound the same.

1. Jean rode her bike down the road.

2. I kept my eye on the ball.

3. Do you write with your right hand or your left?

4. Peter sat in the red chair and read a book.

"And not a creature was stirring— not even a mouse."

Name_____ Date _____

34

Six Whistles

Read the words on the whistles below. Three of the words sound just the same. Color the three whistles that have those words on them.

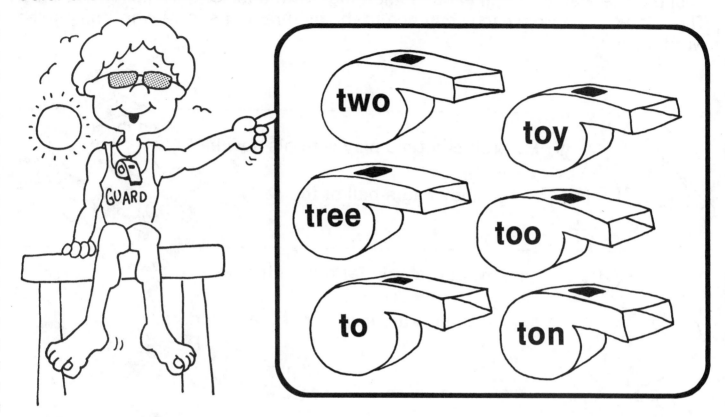

Read the sentences below. Circle the two words in each sentence that sound alike, but look different and mean different things.

1. Jason wants to go swimming at two o'clock.

2. Sarah thinks it's too cold to go swimming.

3. Jason asks Laura if she wants to go swimming too.

4. Laura wants to go with Jason, so the two of them go swimming.

Name_____ Date _____

Have a Ball

Read each pair of sentences. In both sentences there is a word that looks and sounds the same but means something different. Circle the two words. Then draw a line from each sentence to the picture that shows what the circled word means.

My brother let me play with his new ball.

Cindy had a ball at the party.

Kenny saw a ship far out on the water.

Someone used a saw to cut that wood.

I have a puppy who loves to bark.

The bark had been cut in three places.

Terry will have to duck under that branch.

Let's go to the pond and feed the duck.

Name_____ Date _____

36

Park in the Park

Read each pair of sentences below. Find the word in the first sentence that looks and sounds like a word in the second sentence but means something different. Circle the two words. Then draw a line from each sentence to the picture that shows what the circled word means.

Mom found a good place to park.

Let's go to the park and have a picnic.

Jenny dropped her pen on the floor.

The farmer closed the gate of the pen.

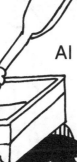

Al learned how to row this summer.

We finished one row and started a new one.

The game ended in a tie.

Anita stopped to tie her shoe.

Name _____ **Date** _____

Match Ups

Read each pair of sentences. In both sentences there is a word that looks and sounds the same but means something different. Circle the two words. Then draw a line from each sentence to the picture that shows what the circled word means.

Sam put his money in the bank.

Marge sat on the bank of the river and read a book.

We saved all the rest for you.

After working hard, it's good to rest.

Eric put the last block in place.

Please don't block the door.

Karen forgot to put a stamp on her letter.

I saw Karen stamp her foot in anger.

Mrs. K. Joyce
1 Park Ave.
N.Y., N.Y.
10006

Name_____ **Date** _____

A Stitch in Time

Read the words below. Then draw a line from each word on the left to the one on the right that sounds just like it.

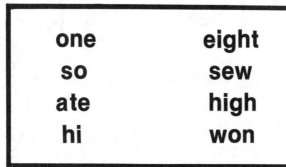

one	eight
so	sew
ate	high
hi	won

Read the sentences below. In each sentence, circle the two words that sound alike, but look different and mean different things.

1. Maria likes to sew, so she made the flag.

2. Our team has won two games and lost one.

3. I can't believe that Bill ate eight apples.

4. From a window high above us,
   a voice called, "Hi."

Name_____ Date _____

Match Mates

Look at the two words in each box. Then look at the two sentences below the box. Write each word in the sentence where it fits.

dear	deer

1. A beautiful _____ stepped out of the forest.

2. My grandmother is very _____ to me.

way	weigh

3. Can you tell me the best _____ to get to Main Street?

4. Does a bag of rocks _____ more than a bag of apples?

bare	bear

5. The grass felt cold under Charlie's _____ feet.

6. The _____ came out of its cave to hunt for food.

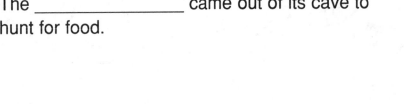

Name_____ **Date** _____

A Rose Is a Rows

Read the words below. Then draw a line from each word on the left to the one on the right that sounds just like it.

hole	**rose**
week	**whole**
sent	**weak**
rows	**cent**

Read the sentences below. In each sentence, circle the two words that sound alike, but look different and mean different things.

1. The hole was so deep that Tom could put his whole arm in it.

2. Judy sent for a book that cost two dollars and one cent.

3. Rhonda always rows the boat with a rose in her hair.

4. Jamal is still feeling weak from having been sick last week.

Sigh... I have no strength.

Name_____ Date _____

Flour Power

Read the two words in each box. Then read the two sentences below the box. Write each word in the sentence where it fits.

meat	**meet**

1. Liz ate her potato, but not her _____ .

2. Dan is going to _____ us at the library after school.

pale	**pail**

3. The baby filled her _____ with sand.

4. Larry painted his boat a _____ blue color.

flour	**flower**

5. Sugar and _____ and eggs are needed to bake a cake.

6. Maria picked a _____ and gave it to her mother.

Name_____   Date _____

A Fish Story

Read the words below. Then draw a line from each word on the left to the one on the right that sounds just like it.

stare	**sale**
fourth	**weight**
sail	**stair**
wait	**forth**

Read the sentences below. In each sentence, circle the two words that sound alike, but look different and mean different things.

1. The army went forth for the fourth time.

2. Kevin got a new sail for his boat at the yard sale.

3. Rosemary stopped on the top stair to stare at a strange sight.

4. Brad can't wait to find out the weight of the fish he caught.

Name_____   Date _____

Grin and Bear It

Read the pairs of sentences below. Find a word in the first sentence that looks and sounds like a word in the second sentence but means something different. Circle the two words that look and sound the same. Then draw a line from each sentence to the box that tells what the circled word means in that sentence.

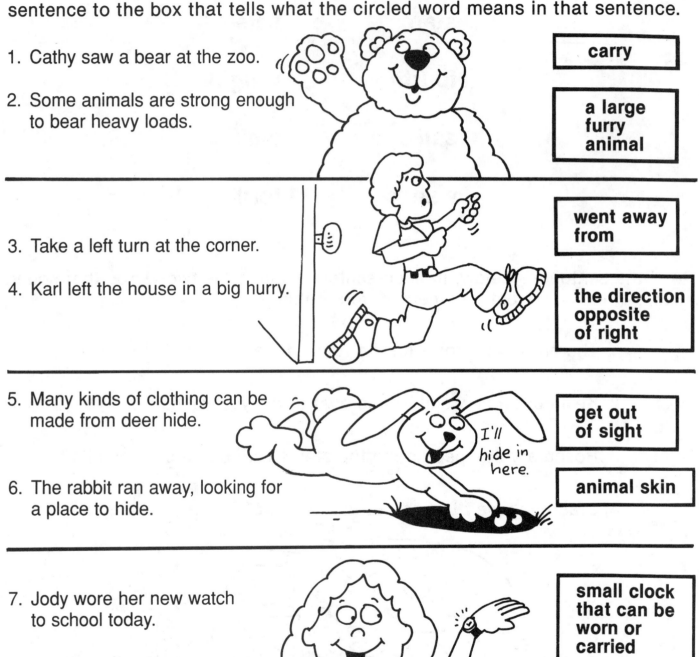

1. Cathy saw a bear at the zoo.

2. Some animals are strong enough to bear heavy loads.

carry

a large furry animal

3. Take a left turn at the corner.

4. Karl left the house in a big hurry.

went away from

the direction opposite of right

5. Many kinds of clothing can be made from deer hide.

6. The rabbit ran away, looking for a place to hide.

get out of sight

animal skin

7. Jody wore her new watch to school today.

8. Jody should watch what the teacher is doing.

small clock that can be worn or carried

look at

Name_____ Date_____

44

Sentence Sets

Read the sentences below. Think about the meaning of the underlined word in each sentence. Then draw a line from each sentence to the picture that goes with it.

Tim *set* the full glass down carefully.

One book is missing from this *set*.

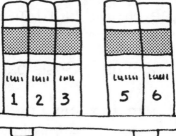

Debbie dropped her cookie on the *ground*.

Pete *ground* up the peanuts to make peanut butter.

A big *wave* made the boat rock.

Emily likes to *wave* to the people who pass.

The children had fun on the rides at the *fair*.

Bonnie said it wasn't *fair* that Sharon had more ice cream.

Name _____ Date _____

An Apple a Day

Read each pair of sentences. Find a word in the first sentence that looks and sounds like a word in the second sentence but means something different. Circle both words. Then draw a line from each sentence to the box that tells what the circled word means.

1. Jim gave Susie part of his apple.

2. Jim and Susie had to part when it was time for dinner.

go away

a piece

3. Mr. Smith sat on a rock to watch the sun go down.

4. Mr. Jones likes to rock in his chair in the evening.

large stone

move back and forth

5. The water level in the lake is low.

6. Martha spoke in a low voice.

WATER LEVEL

HIGH LOW

quiet

not high

7. Scott is a tall, lean boy.

8. Scott likes to lean on the fence.

rest against

thin

Name _____ Date _____

A Summer Drummer

Read the sentences below. Think about the meaning of the underlined word in each sentence. Then draw a line from each sentence to the picture that goes with it.

1. Annie put a rubber _band_ around the papers.

2. My uncle plays the drum in a _band_.

3. Smoke _rose_ up from the fire.

4. The dancer wore a _rose_ in her hair.

5. Ted put lots of _jam_ on his sandwich.

6. All those logs will _jam_ the river.

7. Betsy knows it is wrong to tell a _lie_.

8. Tiny likes to _lie_ on a nice soft couch.

Name _____ Date _____

Go Fly a Kite!

Read each pair of sentences. Look at the underlined word in the first sentence. Find a word in the second sentence that looks just like it but does not sound the same or mean the same thing. Draw a line under that word. Now draw a line from each sentence to the box that tells what the underlined word means and how it sounds in that sentence.

1. The <u>bow</u> of the ship bumped into the dock.

> **MEANING: the front part of a boat or ship**
> **SOUND: rhymes with "now"**

2. Robin Hood shot an arrow from his bow.

> **MEANING: a weapon that shoots arrows**
> **SOUND: rhymes with "go"**

3. A <u>tear</u> ran down Frank's face.

4. Gary didn't mean to tear the paper.

> **MEANING: pull something apart**
> **SOUND: rhymes with "care"**

> **MEANING: drop of water from the eye**
> **SOUND: rhymes with "here"**

> **MEANING: wrap around**
> **SOUND: rhymes with "find"**

5. The <u>wind</u> is blowing hard today.

6. Amy will wind the kite string around a stick.

> **MEANING: air that is moving**
> **SOUND: rhymes with "grinned"**

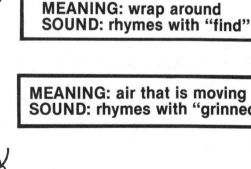

Name_____   Date _____

48

Parade Time

Read each pair of sentences. Look at the underlined word in the first sentence. Find a word in the second sentence that looks just like it but does not sound the same or mean the same thing. Draw a line under that word.

Now draw a line from each sentence to the box that tells what the underlined word means and how it sounds in that sentence.

1. Diane is going to <u>lead</u> the parade.

MEANING: be at the front of
SOUND: rhymes with "need"

2. The pipes are made of lead.

MEANING: a heavy metal
SOUND: rhymes with "bed"

3. We put a pink <u>bow</u> on Fluffy's neck.

MEANING: knotted ribbon
SOUND: rhymes with "go"

4. In our play, we all have to bow to the king.

MEANING: bend over a little
SOUND: rhymes with "cow"

5. Jay fell and got a <u>wound</u> on his leg.

MEANING: wrapped around
SOUND: rhymes with "found"

6. The nurse wound a cloth around Jay's leg.

MEANING: a cut or hurt place
SOUND: rhymes with "tuned"

Name_____ **Date** _____

Boy or Girl?

1. Chris is Marty's sister. Lee is Chris's brother. There are two girls and one boy in their family. Is Marty a girl or a boy? The steps below will help you find out. Circle the right answers.

STEP 1: Chris is Marty's sister. Since Chris
  is a sister, Chris is a _____. **boy   girl**

STEP 2: Lee is Chris's brother. Since Lee is a
  brother, Lee is a _____. **boy   girl**

STEP 3: There are two girls and one boy in the family.
  Look at your answers to Steps 1 and 2. Marty has
  to be a _____. **boy   girl**

2. Jorge is older than Lori. Lori is younger than Julie. Who is youngest? The steps below will help you find out. Circle the right answers.

How old are you?

Lori   Julie

Jorge

STEP 1: Jorge is older than Lori.
  Can Jorge be the youngest?

  Yes   No

STEP 2: Lori is younger than Julie.
  Can Julie be the youngest?

  Yes   No

STEP 3: Look at your answers to Steps 1 and
  2. Which person has to be the youngest?

  Jorge   Lori   Julie

Name_____ Date _____

The Feather Puzzle

Kim found a blue feather. Judy found another feather. Judy's feather was not the same color as Kim's. But Judy's feather was the same color as one of Gary's. Gary had three feathers. One was yellow, one was red, and one was blue.

Judy's feather was the same color as Brian's. Brian's feather was not yellow. What color was Judy's feather?

Does this sound like a hard puzzle? The steps below will help you figure it out. It is not as hard as it sounds!

Read the questions and fill in the answers.

STEP 1: What color is Kim's feather? _____
        Judy's feather is *not* the same color as Kim's.

        So we know that Judy's feather is *not* _____.

STEP 2: Judy's feather is the same color as Brian's.

        Brian's feather is *not* _____.

        So we know that Judy's feather is *not* _____.

STEP 3: Judy's feather is the same color as one of Gary's.
        Gary's feathers are red, yellow, and blue.
        Look at your answers to Steps 1 and 2.
        They tell you two colors that Judy's feather is *not.*

        What color is left? _____

        Color the feathers.

Brian   **Kim**   **Judy**

Name_____ Date _____

Where Do the Periods Belong?

Astronaut Al found a box of moon dots. They are missing from the short stories below. Each story has two or three sentences in it. Every sentence should have a period (moon dot) at the end of it, like this . ⬅

Read each story. Then take your pencil and put a period at the end of each sentence. You should use all the periods in the box.

1. The rocket roared It flew into the clouds

2. Al had eggs for breakfast For lunch he had a sandwich He drank two glasses of milk, too

3. The blast-off was exciting My friends and I watched it on TV

4. Many people would like to go to the moon Amy hopes she can go there Maybe someday Amy's wish will come true

5. Amy went with her father on a train She met Astronaut Al He wrote his name on a piece of paper and gave it to Amy

6. When you come to my house, bring your toy rocket so we can play with it I think that would be fun

Name_____ Date _____

Moon Rocks

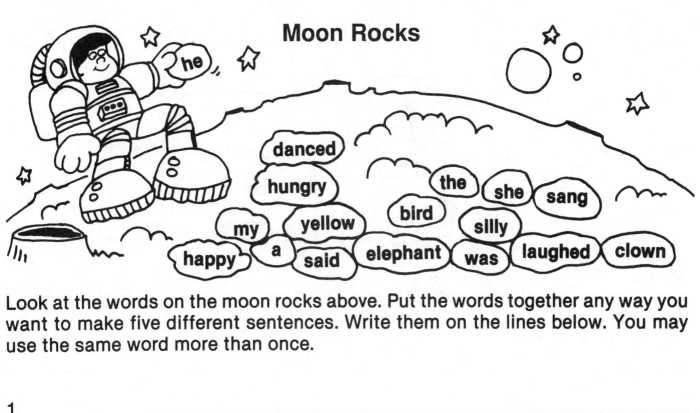

Look at the words on the moon rocks above. Put the words together any way you want to make five different sentences. Write them on the lines below. You may use the same word more than once.

1. _____

_____

2. _____

_____

3. _____

_____

4. _____

_____

5. _____

_____

Name_____ Date _____

A Tale of Rollo

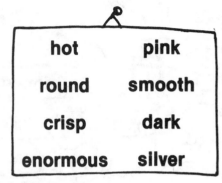

hot	pink
round	smooth
crisp	dark
enormous	silver

Write four funny sentences using any words from the list to tell about Rollo.

1. _____

_____

2. _____

_____

3. _____

_____

4. _____

_____

Circle the words in each sentence that you took from Rollo's list.

Name_____ Date _____

What Is the Question?

? is a sign that a question is being asked. It is called a question mark.

Each sentence below asks a question. Put a question mark at the end of each sentence. Then write the answer to each question on the line.

1. Do you like ice cream _____

2. How old are you _____

3. What color do you like best _____

4. What is your favorite kind of animal _____

5. Do you ever go out at night and look at the stars _____

6. What season of the year do you like best _____

7. What color is your hair _____

8. What color are your eyes _____

Now write a question of your own on the lines below.

_____

_____

Did you remember to end your question with a question mark?

Name_____ Date _____

Question Magic

Sometimes you can make a sentence into a question by changing the words around. Change the words around in each of the sentences below to make a question. Then write the question on the line. Remember to use a question mark. The first one has been done for you.

1. My book is on the table. _____ Is my book on the table? _____

2. Your mother is at work today. _____

3. There are four donkeys in the yard. _____

_____

4. The children didn't want to take their frogs to school. _____

_____

5. You are going to take us to the zoo today. _____

_____

6. These funny little apples are good to eat. _____

_____

7. The scarecrow didn't keep the crows away. _____

_____

8. Barbara can really jump over a high fence. _____

_____

Name_____ Date _____

Sentence Time

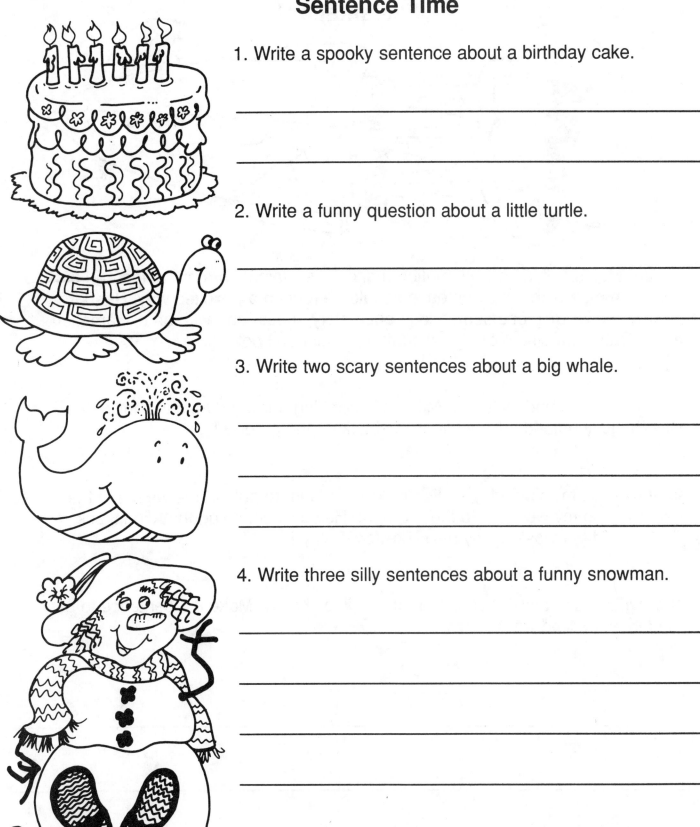

1. Write a spooky sentence about a birthday cake.

_____

_____

2. Write a funny question about a little turtle.

_____

_____

3. Write two scary sentences about a big whale.

_____

_____

_____

4. Write three silly sentences about a funny snowman.

_____

_____

_____

_____

Name_____ Date _____

Exclamation!

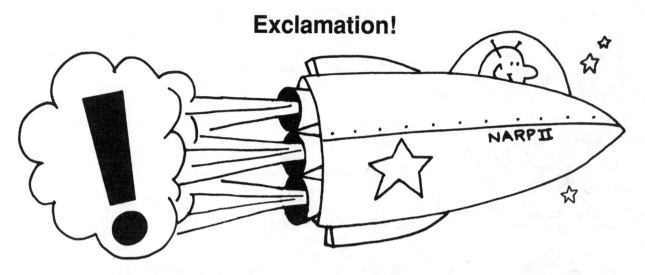

This mark ! is called an exclamation mark. An exclamation mark at the end of a sentence means that the sentence should be read in an excited way. Read the stories below. Only one sentence in each story should end with an exclamation mark. Cross out all the exclamation marks that don't belong.

1. My cat is named Mittens ! Mittens is climbing a tree ! Oh, she's falling ! No, she just jumped ! Now Mittens is back on the ground !

2. It was Timmy's birthday ! His father asked him to pull up the weeds in the garden ! Timmy went out to the garden ! He saw something that didn't look like a weed ! It was a shiny new bike for Timmy !

Now write a sentence of your own on the lines below. Make it a sentence to be read in an excited way.

_____

_____

Remember to end your sentence with an exclamation mark.

Name_____ Date _____

58

Who's Talking?

"Some of these rocks look very
strange," said Al.
Bob told him, "Bring one back
to the ship."

Marks like these " " are called quotation marks. They show that someone is talking. The words between the quotation marks are what the person said. Read the sentences below. Then write the answers in the spaces.

"I have a cat that eats with its tail," said Joan.
Eddie said, "That must be a funny kind of cat."
"All cats eat with their tails, Eddie," Nancy said.
"That's right," said Joan. "They do everything with their
tails. They can't take them off, you know."
Just then Joan's cat came into the room. "Meow,"
it said.

1. Who said the cat must be a funny kind? _____

2. Who said all cats eat with their tails? _____

3. Did one of the children say that cats can't take their tails off?_____

4. Did one of the children say that the cat came into the room? _____

5. What did the cat say? _____

Now write a sentence of your own. The sentence should tell what someone said and who said it. Write it on the lines below. Don't forget the quotation marks.

_____

_____

Name_____ Date _____

The Names Are the Same

Jane, Harry, Cindy, Josh, and **Narp** are all names.

What is the same about them?

All names start with capital letters.

Read the story below. All the names should start with capital letters, but some of them don't. Circle the names that are not right.

The Chair

Kathy told her friend jill about the time six people and a dog all sat in one little chair. First kathy sat in the chair. Then Walter sat down, and then luis. Pretty soon richard came, and he sat there too. Then came Jerry, and last was lisa with her dog, duke. Jill wondered how they all could fit. Do you know?

(The answer is upside-down at the bottom of this page.)

Look at the names you circled above. Write them below the way they should be.

1. _____   2. _____   3. _____

4. _____   5. _____   6. _____

Now write a sentence of your own on the lines below. The sentence should tell about two or more people. Remember to begin their names with capital letters.

_____

_____

They all fit in the chair because each one got up before the next one sat down.

Name_____ Date _____

How It Looks, Feels, and Sounds

Some words help us to understand what things look, feel, or sound like. Look at the words on the rocket. Each word fits into one of the sentences below. Read each sentence. Then pick the word that fits best and write it on the line. Use each word only once.

1. John's hand hurt when it hit the

   _____ wall.

2. The _____ sun shone down

   on the grass and trees.

3. A _____ wind blew as the

   snow began to fall.

4. We had to climb a _____ hill.

5. The _____ music made

   Carrie's ears ring.

6. Sam patted the kitten's _____ fur.

cold

bright

soft

loud

hard

high

Underline the word that best completes each sentence below.

7. Sentence 1 tells how the wall _____.   looks   feels   sounds

8. Sentence 2 tells how the sun _____.   looks   feels   sounds

9. Sentence 3 tells how the wind _____.   looks   feels   sounds

10. Sentence 4 tells how the hill _____.   looks   feels   sounds

11. Sentence 5 tells how the music _____.   looks   feels   sounds

12. Sentence 6 tells how the fur _____.   looks   feels   sounds

Name_____ Date _____

Pick the Right Word

Read the sentences below. Circle the words that tell how something looks, feels, or sounds. Circle one word in each sentence.

1. My blue ball fell into the water.

2. We saw a tiny dog in the yard.

3. Kate filled the cup with warm water.

4. Father sang in a deep voice.

5. A huge truck came down the street.

6. In Al's hand was a round rock.

Read the sentences below. Circle the words that tell how something looks, feels, or sounds. Circle two words in each sentence.

7. A small yellow bird sang in the tree.

8. Jane's dirty face wore a wide smile.

9. The tall girl spoke in a sharp voice.

10. An ugly purple bug was crawling up Tommy's neck.

11. We found a flat place to set down the heavy basket.

12. An orange cat with a long tail sat watching me.

Name_____ **Date** _____

62

Star Paste-Up

Read the sentences below. In each pair, one sentence is right, and the other is not. Cut out the stars at the bottom of the page.

Paste a star next to the sentence that is right in each pair.

	A	**B**

1. ☐ Me and Joe went home.   ☐ Joe and I went home.

2. ☐ We are good friends.   ☐ We is good friends.

3. ☐ Terry and me are going for a ride.   ☐ Terry and I are going for a ride.

4. ☐ Him and me live on the same street.   ☐ He and I live on the same street.

5. ☐ The girls were having a good time.   ☐ The girls was having a good time.

6. ☐ Those are the best apples I ever ate.   ☐ Them are the best apples I ever ate.

Name_____   Date _____

"✂" Cut along the dotted lines.

Right or Wrong?

There aren't no
people or animals on
this here planet.

WRONG ⬜

There aren't
any people or
animals on this
planet.

RIGHT ⬜

Read the sentences below. One sentence is correct in each pair. The other is
not. Pick out the correct sentence in each pair and draw a line under it.

A		B
1. I don't have no candy.	OR	I don't have any candy.
2. Her and me are having a race.	OR	She and I are having a race.
3. I hope she won't beat me in the race.	OR	I hope she won't win me in the race.
4. Lateesha never saw an elephant before.	OR	Lateesha never saw no elephant before.
5. All the children was in their seats.	OR	All the children were in their seats.
6. We didn't feed any pigs.	OR	We didn't feed no pigs.
7. Ellen couldn't see nothing in the dark room.	OR	Ellen couldn't see anything in the dark room.
8. You and me are the only ones who know the secret.	OR	You and I are the only ones who know the secret.

Name_____ **Date** _____

What's the Message?

Toby is sending messages into space. But sometimes he has trouble putting the words in the right order. Read the sentences below and then circle the best answer to each question.

MESSAGE 1: The dog with brown spots ate a bone.
MESSAGE 2: The dog ate a bone with brown spots.

In Message 1, what has spots?	the dog	the bone
In Message 2, what has spots?	the dog	the bone

MESSAGE 3: A man drank some milk in a tall hat.
MESSAGE 4: A man in a tall hat drank some milk.

Which message is about a man drinking from a hat?	3	4
Which message is about a man wearing a hat?	3	4

MESSAGE 5: The girl wearing red boots rode a fast horse.
MESSAGE 6: The girl rode a fast horse wearing red boots.

In Message 5, who is wearing red boots?	the girl	the horse
In Message 6, who is wearing red boots?	the girl	the horse

MESSAGE 7: The little boy found a secret note in the book.
MESSAGE 8: The little boy in the book found a secret note.

In which message does a boy find a note in a book?	7	8
Which message is about a boy in a storybook?	7	8

Name_____ Date _____

Mixed Match-Ups

Narp thinks that Kevin means his little brother is *really* a peanut.

We know that Kevin means his brother is small, *like* a peanut.

Look at the sentences below. Read a sentence on the left. Then find a sentence on the right that tells what it means. Draw a line to match the sentences. Match the other sentences the same way.

He is an oak tree.   He runs fast.

He is a turtle.   He is tall and strong.

He is a mule.   He is very slow.

He is an eagle.   He has sharp eyes.

He is a rabbit.   He doesn't do anything
                                       he doesn't want to do.

Name_____   **Date** _____

Fill in the Blanks

Look at the words on the rocket. Each word fits into one of the sentences below it. Read each sentence. Then pick the word that fits best in each sentence. Write the word on the line.

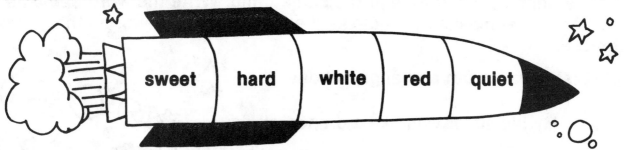

1. The ice was like a rock. The ice was _____.

2. This morning the baby was like a little mouse. This morning the baby

   was _____.

3. The man's nose was like a cherry. The man's nose was _____.

4. The ripe fruit tasted like candy. The ripe fruit was _____.

5. Grandma's hair was like snow. Grandma's hair was _____.

Narp wants you to pick the word that best fits each sentence below. Write the word on the line.

green	gentle	slowly	silly	deep

6. Tom says his big dog is really as _____ as a lamb.

7. The hole in our yard looks as _____ as the ocean.

8. Sometimes Alan is as _____ as a clown.

9. My new shirt is as _____ as grass.

10. Karen walks as _____ as a turtle.

Name_____ Date _____

Same or Different

Read the first sentence below. Under it are two more sentences. One of them says the same thing as the first sentence, but in a more interesting way. The other sentence does not mean the same thing. Write the word **same** next to the sentence that means the same as the first one. Do this for all the groups of sentences.

1. My big sister was mean and angry all day.

a. _____ My big sister was like a dragon all day.

b. _____ My big sister was like a sheep all day.

2. After our fight, we didn't get along very well.

a. _____ After our fight, we built a bridge between us.

b. _____ After our fight, there was a wall between us.

3. There were a lot of papers flying around in the air.

a. _____ There was a mountain of paper.

b. _____ There was a snowstorm of paper.

4. Spot was so happy his eyes shone.

a. _____ Spot had stars in his eyes.

b. _____ Spot had streams in his eyes.

5. He could do anything with his strong hands.

a. _____ He could do anything with his glass hands.

b. _____ He could do anything with his iron hands.

Name_____ Date _____

Sentence Fun

The teacher asked the children to finish the sentence below. Each child had a different idea. Some of them are shown below. You may have an idea of your own. Write your idea on the line.

Her hands were *as warm as* _____.

a kitten   **tea**   **an oven**   **oatmeal**   **a summer day**

Read each sentence below. Then write one or more words on the line to finish the sentence.

1. Wendy's eyes are as blue as _____.

2. My uncle is so tall that he is like _____.

3. The knock on the door was as loud as _____.

4. We ran here and there like _____.

5. This dog is as lazy as _____.

6. The lion's teeth were as sharp as_____.

7. After his swim, Kenny felt as cool as _____.

8. Today I feel as strong as_____.

Name_____ **Date** _____

Think & Write

as small as my thumb

Write a sentence on the lines below. Use the words given above in your sentence. Or make up an "as _____ as _____" idea of your own to use.

_____

_____

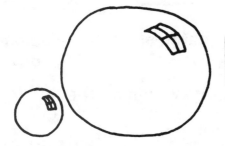

like a bubble

Write a sentence on the lines below. Use the words given above in your sentence. Or make up a "like _____" idea of your own to use.

_____

_____

as big as an elephant

Write a sentence on the lines below. Use the words given above in your sentence. Or make up an "as _____ as _____" idea of your own to use.

_____

_____

Name_____ Date _____

The Strange Planet

You and your friend have landed on a strange planet. No person has ever been there before. What kinds of things do you think you might see? What kinds of things might happen to you?

Write a story on the lines below that tells about your adventures on the new planet. Tell how things look, feel, and sound. Tell how you and your friend feel. Tell what you do. Use the back of this paper if you need more space.

My Adventures on a Strange Planet

_____

_____

_____

_____

_____

_____

_____

Name_____ Date _____

Make Up a Story

Draw a picture in the space above. Then write a story about your picture on the lines below. Put the name of your story on the top line. Use the back of this paper if you need more space.

_____

Name_____ **Date** _____

Let's Play

Imagine that you are inventing a new game. You can make up all the rules. Name the equipment and positions whatever you like, as long as the names make sense. In the space below, explain how to play your new game.

_____

_____

_____

_____

_____

_____

_____

_____

_____

_____

_____

_____

_____

_____

Name_____ **Date** _____

The Birthday Party

Jennifer invited all her friends to her birthday party. When they arrived, they were surprised to see Jennifer crying. Use some of the action words below to tell what happened.

fall	bark	fix
break	crash	jump
tumble	splash	climb

_____

_____

_____

_____

_____

_____

_____

_____

_____

_____

_____

_____

_____

Name_____ **Date** _____